Y0-BDH-176

NATIONAL
GEOGRAPHIC
KiDS

weird
but
true!

SPORTS

NATIONAL
GEOGRAPHIC
KiDS

Weird but true!

SPORTS

300 wacky facts about awesome athletics

NATIONAL GEOGRAPHIC
WASHINGTON, D.C.

"IF YOU DARE!"

4

YOU CAN WATER-SKI WHILE BEING TOWED BY AN AIRPLANE.

THE WINNER OF THE FRENCH-LANGUAGE SCRABBLE WORLD CHAMPIONSHIP DOESN'T SPEAK FRENCH.

More than **1,200 games** of **marbles** are played in **just four days** during the annual National Marbles Tournament.

IT IS ESTIMATED THAT IF THE HOT DOGS GAMES EACH YEAR WERE LINED UP,

7,827 EMPIRE

A bike traveling at least eight miles an hour (13 km/h) can keep going without a rider.

EATEN AT MAJOR LEAGUE BASEBALL THEY WOULD STRETCH AS LONG AS

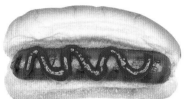  

STATE BUILDINGS.

**AMERICA'S FIRST
FEMALE OLYMPIC CHAMPION
COMPETED AGAINST HER OWN
MOTHER—AND WON.**

THE RECORD FOR THE MOST

SURF'S UP, DOG!

DOGS ON A SURFBOARD?

17

A NASCAR PIT CREW **CAN CHANGE ALL FOUR TIRES AND** FILL A CAR'S GAS TANK **IN LESS THAN 15 SECONDS.**

The same material used to make **bulletproof vests** is also found in **hockey sticks.**

WINNERS OF A *PAALZITTEN* (POLE SITTING) COMPETITION SPENT 87 HOURS AND 52 MINUTES ON THEIR LOFTY PERCHES—TAKING BREAKS ONLY TO USE THE BATHROOM.

A pro basketball player was fined **$25,000** for throwing his used **mouth guard** into the stands.

A baseball player's decades-old used **toothpick** sold at auction for **$440.**

THE **AQUATIC CENTER** BUILT FOR THE 2012 **LONDON OLYMPICS** HAS A **STINGRAY-SHAPED ROOF.**

ACTUAL STINGRAY!

14

KITE FIGHTING
IS A NATIONAL SPORT
IN THAILAND.

15

SPEED BRICK BREAKER KEVIN TAYLOR **SMASHED** 584 CEMENT BRICKS IN LESS THAN **A MINUTE** USING ONLY **HIS HANDS.**

Villagers in 5th-century Italy played tennis with their bare hands.

MOST CONCRETE PATIO BLOCKS BROKEN BY A SINGLE STRIKE OF THE ELBOW?

17

IT TOOK
LESS
THAN AN
HOUR
FOR A MAN TO
POGO-STICK
UP THE
1,899 STEPS
OF THE
CN TOWER
IN ONTARIO,
CANADA.

PEOPLE USING
EXTREME
**POGO
STICKS**
**BOUNCE
SO HIGH** THEY
CAN DO FLIPS.

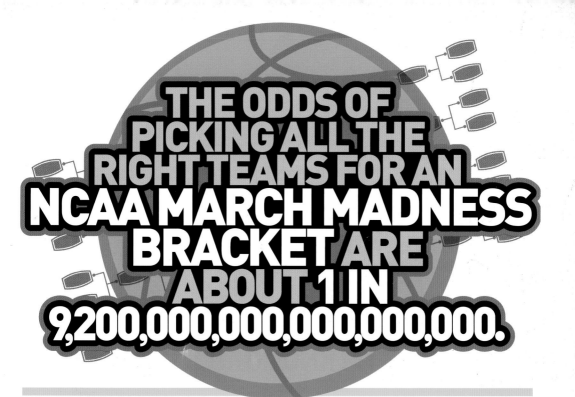

THE ODDS OF PICKING ALL THE RIGHT TEAMS FOR AN **NCAA MARCH MADNESS** BRACKET ARE ABOUT 1 IN **9,200,000,000,000,000,000.**

UKRAINIAN ATHLETE SERGEY BUBKA BROKE MEN'S POLE-VAULT WORLD RECORDS **(INCLUDING HIS OWN!)** 35 TIMES DURING HIS CAREER.

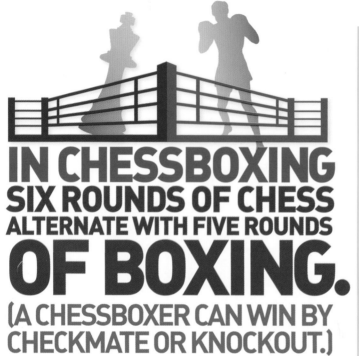

IN CHESSBOXING
SIX ROUNDS OF CHESS
ALTERNATE WITH FIVE ROUNDS
OF BOXING.
(A CHESSBOXER CAN WIN BY CHECKMATE OR KNOCKOUT.)

A COMPANY DESIGNED SWIMMING FLIPPERS THAT MIMIC A HUMPBACK WHALE'S FIN.

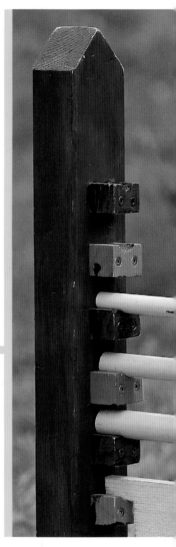

BUNNIES COMPETING IN THE RABBIT GRAND NATIONAL IN NORTH YORKSHIRE, ENGLAND, ARE SPECIALLY **TRAINED TO LEAP OVER HURDLES.**

A STUDY FOUND THAT A 3-HOUR BASEBALL GAME INVOLVES AN AVERAGE OF JUST 18 MINUTES OF ACTUAL PLAY TIME.

SOME HOCKEY GAMES
ARE PLAYED ON
UNICYCLES.

Tennis balls are covered in **fuzzy felt** so that they travel slower and are easier to control.

SUMMER
OLYMPICS
HELD SOUTH OF THE
EQUATOR ACTUALLY
**TAKE PLACE DURING
THE HOST COUNTRY'S**
WINTER.

OLYMPIC GOLD MEDALIST BRYAN CLAY

YANKED HIS DAUGHTER'S LOOSE TOOTH

BY TYING IT TO HIS **JAVELIN** BEFORE THROWING IT.

Ballet began as a weapons-free interpretation of *fencing*.

25

Early **bicycles** were known as **hobby-horses.**

Five-time NBA MVP **Michael Jordan** was cut from his high school basketball team.

AN ARCHITECT PROPOSED A DESIGN

FOR AN UNDERWATER
TENNIS COURT

OFF THE COAST OF
DUBAI, UNITED
ARAB EMIRATES.

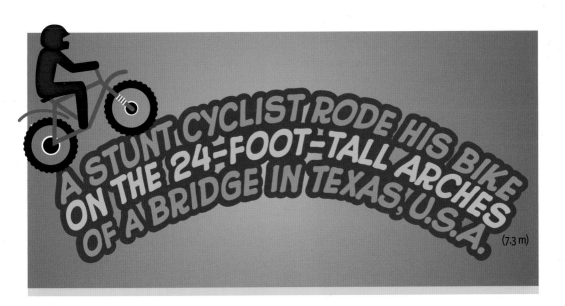

A STUNT CYCLIST RODE HIS BIKE ON THE 24-FOOT-TALL ARCHES OF A BRIDGE IN TEXAS, U.S.A. (7.3 m)

ANCIENT GREEK OLYMPIANS THREW **JAVELINS** FROM HORSEBACK.

Jousting lasted for more than **400 years** *in Europe, but there are now only some* **200 competitive** *jousters around the world.*

TENNIS STAR MARiA SHARAPOVA'S

ON-COURT, BALL-HITTING GRUNTS

HAVE REACHED **101 DECIBELS,** AS NOISY AS A PASSING **MOTORCYCLE.**

AT FENWAY PARK IN BOSTON, MASSACHUSETTS, U.S.A., FANS GOBBLE ABOUT **1,000 bags of** Cracker Jack EACH GAME.

AT AN ANNUAL COMPETITION IN COXHEATH, U.K.,

COSTUME-WEARING TEAMS

34

HURL CUSTARD PIES
AT EACH OTHER.

35

The women's world-record-setting **hammer throw** soared **266 feet**— (81.08 m) more than **four times** the length of a **bowling lane.**

THE HIGHEST **A HOT AIR BALLOON**

HAS EVER FLOWN WAS MORE THAN

69,000 (21,031 m) FEET—

ABOUT **25 TIMES HIGHER** THAN THE WORLD'S TALLEST BUILDING.

★ ★ ★ ★ ★
NATIONALS PARK
IN WASHINGTON, D.C., U.S.A.,
OFFERED FANS A
BURGER WEIGHING
EIGHT POUNDS—
AS MUCH AS A (3.5 kg)
SMALL BOWLING BALL.
★ ★ ★ ★ ★ ★ ★ ★ ★ ★ ★

Olympic gold medals aren't actually made of gold. (They're mostly silver.)

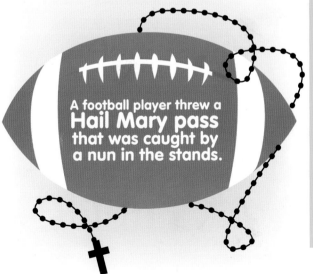

A football player threw a **Hail Mary pass** that was caught by a nun in the stands.

14,625 =
the record
for most holes
of golf
played by one
person in one year.

37

A **surfer** in Portugal once caught a **wave** taller than a **six-story** building.

THE AVERAGE NFL TEAM PRODUCES SOME **5,500 POUNDS** OF LAUNDRY (2,495 kg) PER WEEK.

Roller soccer = soccer played on skates.

Baseballs have hit Fenway Park's left-field wall so hard the **dents** have **stitch marks.**

ATHLETES IN THE IRONMAN TRIATHLON SWIM 2.4 MILES, (3.9 km) BIKE 112 MILES, (180 km) AND RUN A FULL 26.2-MILE (42-km) MARATHON.

People in Boulder, Colorado, U.S.A., ride inner tubes to the office on Tube to Work Day.

ANCIENT EGYPTIANS **FENCED** WITH STICKS.

A 14-YEAR-OLD BOY LAUNCHED AN **ARROW** THE LENGTH OF FOUR AND A HALF FOOTBALL FIELDS.

BOXING CHAMPION DANNY GARCIA **CHASED CHICKENS** AROUND THE RING TO WORK ON HIS **QUICKNESS.**

The Chicago White Sox sell a 12-scoop banana split at their stadium. It's served in a full-size batting helmet.

BIATHLON—
A SPORT THAT COMBINES
SKIING AND **TARGET SHOOTING—**
BEGAN AS A TRAINING ACTIVITY FOR
NORWEGIAN SOLDIERS.

When **divers** practice new tricks, they use a **bubble machine** to "**soften**" the water's surface.

Professional **badminton players** can smash **shuttlecocks** as fast as

200 miles (322 km/h) **an hour.**

A SHUTTLECOCK HAS **16 GOOSE FEATHERS**— ALL TAKEN FROM THE **BIRD'S** LEFT WING.

A PERSON WHO IS WALKING USES **SIX TIMES MORE ENERGY** THAN A CYCLIST RIDING AT THE SAME SPEED.

A British strongman has balanced bunk beds, refrigerators, and cars on his head.

BASEBALL STAR TY COBB'S
TEETH
SOLD AT AUCTION FOR
$7,475.

Professional **hockey players** can be **penalized** for tucking their jerseys into their pants.

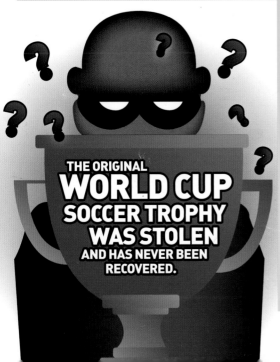

THE ORIGINAL
WORLD CUP SOCCER TROPHY WAS STOLEN
AND HAS NEVER BEEN RECOVERED.

49

MAJOR LEAGUE BASEBALL PITCHER TURK WENDELL BRUSHED HIS TEETH BETWEEN INNINGS.

BOXER MANNY PACQUIAO AVERAGES 2,500 SIT-UPS A DAY WHILE IN TRAINING CAMP.

At the annual **Pancake Race** in the town of **Olney, U.K.,** runners **sprint** beside each other while holding **frying pans** and **flapjacks.**

In gymnastics a **twisting** **double** **somersault** on a trampoline is called a **fliffis.**

51

GLACIER CAVES ARE CONSTANTLY CHANGING,

SO THEY ARE **DIFFERENT** EVERY TIME CAVERS **EXPLORE** THEM.

A man in Texas, U.S.A., **plays golf with a club** longer than **two Smart cars.**

20.5 FEET (6.2 M)

A BRITISH MAN ONCE LIFTED A STACK OF BOOKS WEIGHING MORE THAN 35 POUNDS (16 kg) WITH HIS EYE SOCKET.

A WOMAN ONCE SET A **WORLD RECORD** BY **TOSSING A ROLLING PIN** MORE THAN HALF THE LENGTH OF A **PROFESSIONAL SOCCER FIELD.**

A hockey player once autographed a fan's already-bitten **grilled cheese sandwich.**

A Slovenian man **cycled more** than **561 miles** (903.76 km) in **24 hours.**

That's like biking more than **21 marathons** in one day!

55

BASE
jumper
Lonnie Bissonnette's
wheelchair
has its own
parachute.

Many professional **cyclists** ride far enough in a single year to travel from New York City to Los Angeles **ten times.**

YOU COULD SEE THE STADIUM LIGHTS OF THE 2014 WORLD CUP FROM SPACE.

PITTSBURGH, PENNSYLVANIA, IS THE ONLY U.S. CITY **THAT HAS THE SAME COLORS** (BLACK AND GOLD) FOR ALL OF ITS MAJOR **SPORTS TEAMS.**

AN AUSTRALIAN MARATHON RUNNER ONCE HAD A **BUTLER** CYCLE ALONGSIDE HIM WITH FOOD AND WATER.

Getting **three strikes in a row in bowling** is called a **"turkey"** because people used to win **live birds** when they did.

59

IN **ARCHERY GOLF,** PLAYERS HIT BALLS WITH **ARROWS** INSTEAD OF **CLUBS.**

AN 11-YEAR-OLD BOY ONCE DID 84 BARANIS (SOMERSAULTS WITH A HALF TWIST) **IN ONE MINUTE ON A TRAMPOLINE.**

THE WORLD'S LARGEST ROCK PAPER SCISSORS TOURNAMENT INVOLVED 2,950 PARTICIPANTS.

A **4,800-** (2,177-kg) **pound red apple** pops up from behind the center-field **fence** every time a **New York Mets player** hits a **home run.**

THE OLYMPIC TORCH HAS BEEN TO SPACE.

Some people use bathtubs as kayaks.

BASKETBALL PLAYER WILT CHAMBERLAIN
ONCE SCORED **100 POINTS**
IN A SINGLE GAME.

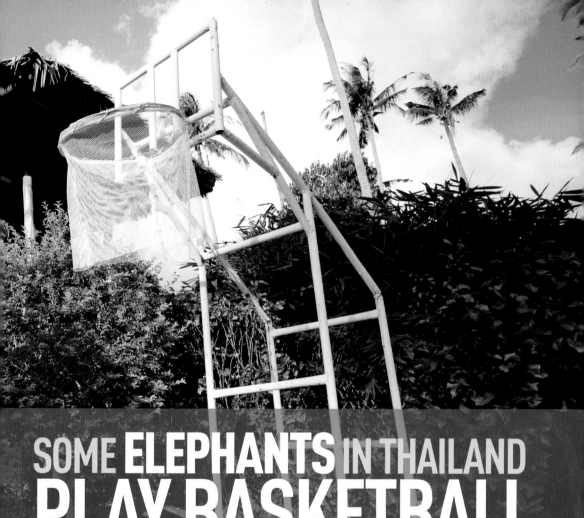

SOME **ELEPHANTS** IN THAILAND **PLAY BASKETBALL.**

A HERD OF COWS WANDERED ONTO THE CYCLISTS' ROUTE DURING THE 2015 TOUR DE FRANCE.

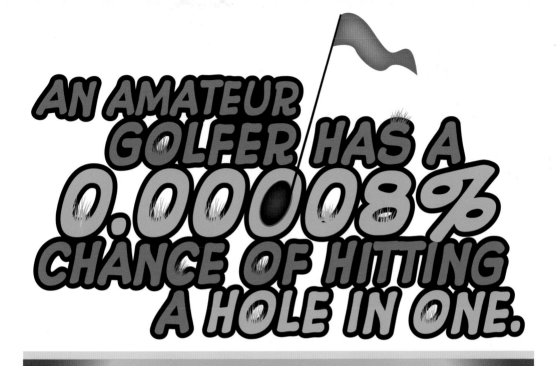

AN AMATEUR GOLFER HAS A 0.00008% CHANCE OF HITTING A HOLE IN ONE.

A **NINE-YEAR-OLD** BOY FROM BELGIUM DID **1,321** CARTWHEELS IN LESS THAN **38 MINUTES.**

OCTOPUS WRESTLING

WAS ONCE A POPULAR SPORT IN TACOMA, WASHINGTON, U.S.A.

AT A COUNTY FAIR IN OREGON, U.S.A., DRIVERS RACE FORD MODEL Ts WHILE HOLDING **SQUEALING PIGS.**

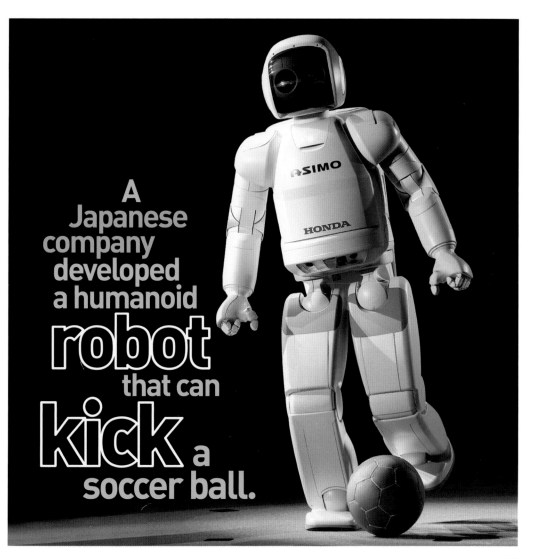

A Japanese company developed a humanoid **robot** that can **kick** a soccer ball.

After all three of his **wins at Wimbledon,** a Serbian tennis pro celebrated by **eating grass** off the court.

54,250 = THE NUMBER OF BALLS

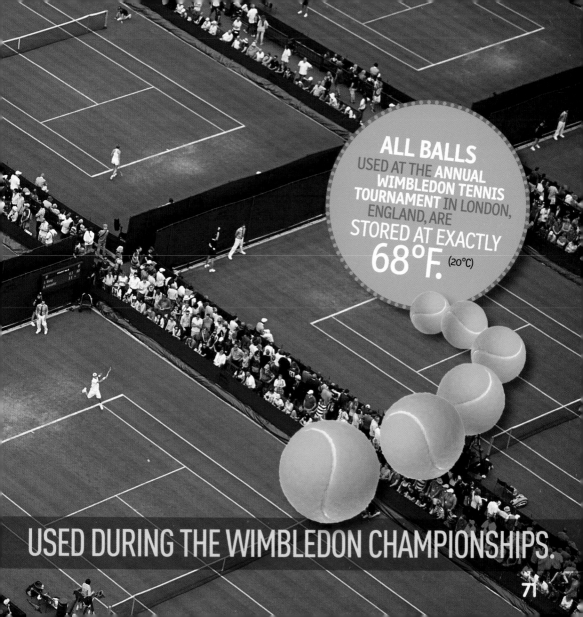

ALL BALLS USED AT THE ANNUAL WIMBLEDON TENNIS TOURNAMENT IN LONDON, ENGLAND, ARE STORED AT EXACTLY **68°F.** (20°C)

USED DURING THE WIMBLEDON CHAMPIONSHIPS.

ICE HOCKEY

WAS ONCE AN EVENT IN THE SUMMER OLYMPICS.

Researchers have come up with a **wearable air bag** for skiers that will deploy if they **crash** on the slopes.

When **cheerleading** first started, it was for **men only.**

In the
1988 and 1992
Winter Olympics,
ski-ballet
competitors **jumped,**
flipped, and danced to music
while skiing downhill.

In 1914 a dog named **Toots** became famous for playing pool with his **nose.**

DURING THE MEGAVALANCHE MOUNTAIN BIKE RACE IN THE FRENCH ALPS, SOME 2,700 RIDERS CAREEN TWO MILES (3.3 km) DOWN A SUPER-SLIPPERY GLACIER.

Swimmer **Michael Phelps** has **won more** Olympic **medals** than most **countries** have.

11 HOURS =

LENGTH OF THE LONGEST WRESTLING MATCH

IN OLYMPIC HISTORY.

The **mud** that's rubbed on **major league baseballs** before play comes from **one specific spot** in New Jersey, U.S.A.

NO ONE WILL SAY EXACTLY WHERE THAT SPOT IS.

A motorcycle driver sat on the **handlebars** while doing a **108-mile-per-hour wheelie.** (174-km/h)

A 61-YEAR-OLD AUSTRALIAN POTATO FARMER ONCE WON A **543.7-MILE** (875-km) ULTRAMARATHON AFTER DOING MOST OF HIS TRAINING IN RAIN BOOTS.

Piglets paddle across a pool, play "pigball," and run races in the **Pig Olympics** in Moscow, Russia.

81

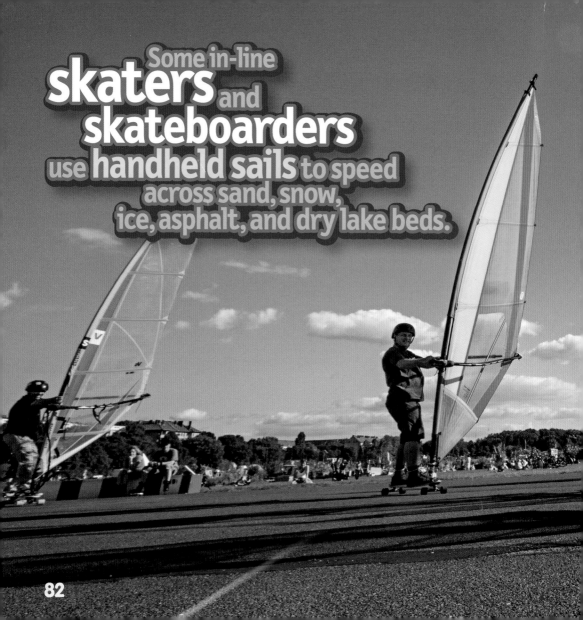

Some in-line **skaters** and **skateboarders** use **handheld sails** to speed across sand, snow, ice, asphalt, and dry lake beds.

JOGGLING=

RUNNING WHILE CONTINUOUSLY JUGGLING AT LEAST THREE BALLS.

THE WORLD'S LONGEST GOLF COURSE IS 848 MILES LONG (1,365 km) AND SPANS TWO TIME ZONES.

THE LONGEST SKIS IN THE WORLD

STRETCHED MORE THAN **1,820 FEET** (555 m)

AND WERE WORN BY **170 SKIERS.**

A COMPETITIVE EATER NICKNAMED **MEGATOAD** SET A WORLD RECORD BY INGESTING **182 SLICES OF BACON** IN **FIVE MINUTES.**

A WORLD CUP-WINNING **GOALKEEPER** INSURED HIS HANDS FOR MORE THAN **FOUR MILLION DOLLARS.**

85

A Belgian man set a world record for the most **swim caps** worn at one time: **75.**

EVENING GAMES PLAYED AT A **WEST-FACING** BASEBALL STADIUM IN PITTSFIELD, MASSACHUSETTS, U.S.A., NEED TEMPORARY **"SUN DELAYS"** BECAUSE THE RAYS CAN BE SO BLINDING TO HITTERS.

Runner **Fauja Singh** completed a **marathon** at the age of **101.**

THE MEANINGS OF THE YELLOW AND RED PENALTY CARDS IN SOCCER WERE INSPIRED BY TRAFFIC-LIGHT COLORS.

Every **player** on the 1994 **Bulgarian** World Cup soccer team had a **last name** ending with the letters **OV.**

A college basketball game was played on an aircraft carrier.

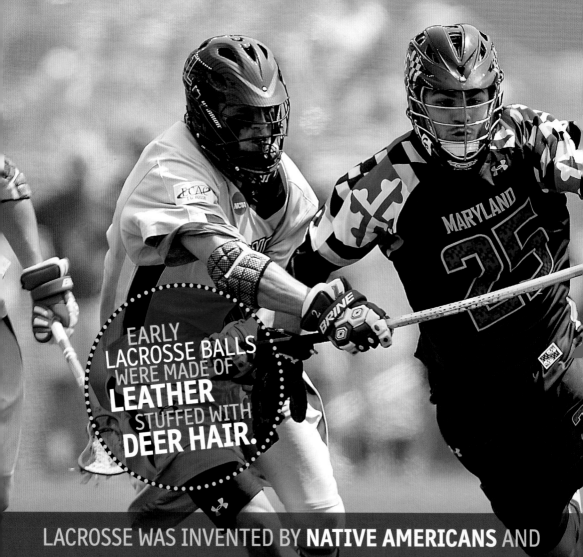

EARLY LACROSSE BALLS WERE MADE OF **LEATHER** STUFFED WITH **DEER HAIR.**

LACROSSE WAS INVENTED BY **NATIVE AMERICANS** AND

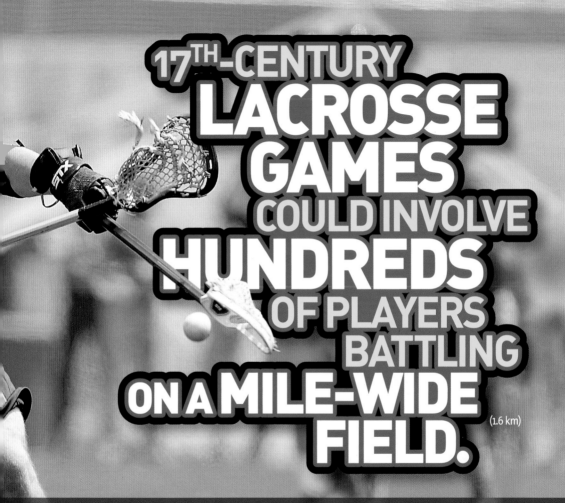

17TH-CENTURY LACROSSE GAMES COULD INVOLVE HUNDREDS OF PLAYERS BATTLING ON A MILE-WIDE FIELD. (1.6 km)

WAS ONCE USED AS A WAY TO SETTLE **DISPUTES** AMONG TRIBES.

TENNIS BALLS
USED TO BE BLACK OR WHITE. THEY WERE CHANGED TO YELLOW WHEN IT WAS DISCOVERED THAT TV VIEWERS COULD SEE THEM BETTER.

THIRTY SNOOZEBOXES—INFLATABLE PODS BIG ENOUGH TO FIT A BED—WERE SET UP BESIDE A **WELSH SOCCER TEAM'S FIELD** SO PLAYERS COULD **REST** BETWEEN TRAINING SESSIONS.

Intentionally kicking another player's shins in soccer is called **HACKING.**

EACH YEAR, THOUSANDS OF PEOPLE **JOiN A NAKED BiKE RiDE** IN PORTLAND, OREGON, U.S.A.

THE MOST PEOPLE IN A SINGLE CANOE: **143**

SOME **CHAMPION RACEHORSES** HAVE BEEN **CLONED.**

A British woman **swam** the length of two soccer fields underwater without coming up for air.

SOME ROCK CLIMBERS **SLEEP IN TENTS HANGING** FROM THE SIDE OF A **CLIFF.**

TWO MEN FREE-CLIMBED 3,000 VERTICAL FEET — (914 m) **MORE THAN FIVE TIMES HIGHER THAN THE WASHINGTON MONUMENT — USING ONLY THEIR HANDS, THEIR FEET, AND SAFETY EQUIPMENT TO STOP A FALL.**

ROCK CLIMBERS OFTEN HAVE THICKER FINGER BONES THAN OTHER PEOPLE.

YOU CAN TURN YOUR COUCH INTO A BICYCLE.

A SCHOOL OF FISH ONCE JUMPED OUT OF A LAKE **AND INTO THE BOAT** OF A COLLEGE ROWING TEAM **IN MISSOURI, U.S.A.**

AT THE 1904 OLYMPICS A MARATHON RUNNER STOPPED AT AN *ORCHARD* TO PICK APPLES— AND STILL FINISHED IN **FOURTH PLACE.**

IT TOOK AN **ULTRA-**MARATHONER **46 DAYS,** 8 HOURS, AND 7 MINUTES TO **HIKE** THE **2,189** (3,523 km) MILES OF THE APPALACHIAN **TRAIL.** (THAT'S MORE THAN **47 MILES** A DAY!) (76 km)

Players literally **bounce** off the walls while playing **trampoline dodgeball.**

Pro basketball player Reggie Miller once scored **8** points in **9** seconds.

DURING A RAINY MATCH, **A TENNIS STAR PLAYED WHILE HOLDING AN** UMBRELLA IN ONE HAND AND HIS **RACKET** IN THE OTHER.

Golf is the only sport that has been played on the **moon**.

99

IN **INDONESIA,** *PACU JAWI* JOCKEYS RIDE A **PLOW** BETWEEN **TWO** **RUNNING BULLS** TO **"MUD SKI"** ACROSS FLOODED **RICE FIELDS.**

AN **ITALIAN UNDERWATER CYCLIST** RODE HIS BIKE **218 FEET** BELOW THE (66 m) **OCEAN'S SURFACE.**

The biggest cheerleading cheer was performed by 1,278 people at once.

The world's highest BASE jump started near the top of Mount Everest—at 23,688 feet (7,220 m) above sea level.

NBA player Luke Ridnour was a member of four different teams in just 25 hours.

103

BIRDS USED IN **FALCONRY** **WEAR HOODS** WHEN THEY ARE NOT HUNTING.

THE **KAZAKH PEOPLE OF MONGOLIA** HAVE BEEN HUNTING WITH **GOLDEN EAGLES** FOR **2,000 YEARS.**

Two hang gliders set a distance record by flying more than 470 miles (756 km) through Texas, U.S.A., without stopping.

105

ACTUAL PRISON BREAKS INSPIRED THE *ESCAPE FROM ALCATRAZ TRIATHLON* IN CALIFORNIA, U.S.A., WHERE COMPETITORS LEAP OFF A BOAT AND SWIM ACROSS SAN FRANCISCO BAY.

At a college in Vermont, U.S.A., graduating students **ski downhill** wearing their **caps and gowns.**

SPLASH HITS = HOME-RUN BALLS HIT BY SAN FRANCISCO GIANTS PLAYERS THAT LAND IN THE BAY OUTSIDE THE STADIUM.

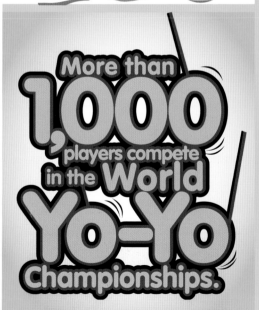

More than 1,000 players compete in the World Yo-Yo Championships.

SOCHI, RUSSIA, OLYMPIC ORGANIZERS STOCKPILED enough artificial snow for the games TO BE SEEN FROM SPACE.

The world's fastest
lawn mower—
the
Mean Mower—
can travel
116 miles
an hour (187 km/h)
when not
on grass.

HONDA

www.honda.co.uk

SOME PROFESSIONAL
GOLF CADDIES CAN EARN UP TO
ONE MILLION DOLLARS
IN A SEASON.

AN AUSTRALIAN WATER POLO PLAYER STICKS HER **CHEWED GUM** UNDER A CHAIR OR UNDER THE GOAL **BEFORE EVERY MATCH.**

The steering wheel of a **Formula One race car** has more than **35 buttons,** levers, lights, dials, and switches.

WORLD CUP MASCOTS

HAVE INCLUDED

A **STICK FIGURE,**

A **SMILING ORANGE,**

A SOMBRERO-WEARING **CHILI PEPPER,**

AND A **TRIO** OF **ALIENS.**

GYMNASTICS BALANCE BEAMS

ABOUT THE WIDTH

ARE ONLY 4 INCHES WIDE—
(10 cm)

OF A BRICK. ➘

A MAN DROVE A CAR 1.16 MILES (1.87 km) IN TWO MINUTES AND TEN SECONDS—ON ONLY ITS RIGHT TWO WHEELS.

AN OLYMPIC ROWER ONCE LOST HIS GOLD MEDAL AT THE BOTTOM OF A MUDDY RIVER AFTER LEAPING INTO THE WATER TO CELEBRATE HIS VICTORY.

A **polar bear** at the San Diego Zoo can dribble a **basketball** underwater.

Usain Bolt— the world's fastest man— ate an average of **100 chicken nuggets a day** during the Beijing Olympics, where he won **three gold medals.**

The tennis term "love" (meaning a zero score) is thought to come from a mispronunciation of *l'oeuf*—the French word for "egg."

Some of the first British **surfers** used **coffin lids** to ride the **waves.**

ZANY MASCOTS

THE FIGHTING PICKLE=
UNIVERSITY OF NORTH CAROLINA SCHOOL OF THE ARTS, NORTH CAROLINA, U.S.A.

THE TROLL=
TRINITY COLLEGE, ILLINOIS, U.S.A.

THE TREE =
STANFORD UNIVERSITY,
CALIFORNIA, U.S.A.

THE DEMON DEACON =
WAKE FOREST UNIVERSITY,
NORTH CAROLINA, U.S.A.

THE BANANA SLUG =
UNIVERSITY OF CALIFORNIA,
SANTA CRUZ, CALIFORNIA, U.S.A.

A WOMAN CRUSHED A RECORD-SETTING **TEN APPLES** IN ONE MINUTE— **WITH HER BICEPS.**

SAN FRANCISCO, CALIFORNIA, U.S.A., has a special **court** where people can play **polo** on bicycles.

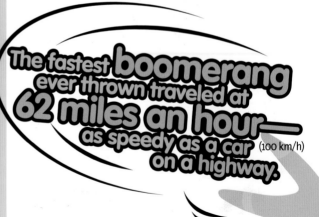

The fastest **boomerang** ever thrown traveled at **62 miles an hour—** as speedy as a car (100 km/h) on a highway.

YOU CAN WATCH OSTRICH RACES IN SOUTH AFRICA.

WINNERS OF A MEXICAN **TENNIS TOURNAMENT** TAKE HOME A **TROPHY** SHAPED LIKE A **GIANT PEAR.**

IN THE **INDIAN** GAME OF *KABADDI,* A "**RAIDER**" HAS TO **TAG** THE OPPOSING TEAM'S PLAYERS WHILE **CHANTING** AND HOLDING HIS BREATH.

122

SOME HOCKEY FANS THROW DEAD FISH, OCTOPUSES, SLABS OF BEEF, AND RUBBER RATS ONTO THE ICE WHEN THEIR TEAM SCORES A GOAL.

Powerboating was an Olympic sport for the first— and last—time at the 1908 games.

OLYMPIC TRAMPOLINE COMPETITORS CAN SOAR MORE THAN **33 FEET** (10 m) IN THE AIR—AS HIGH AS A SCHOOL BUS IS LONG.

123

Professional dragon-boat racers can row the length of 4.5 football fields in just two minutes.

The
average
life span
of an
NBA basketball
is about

10,000
bounces.

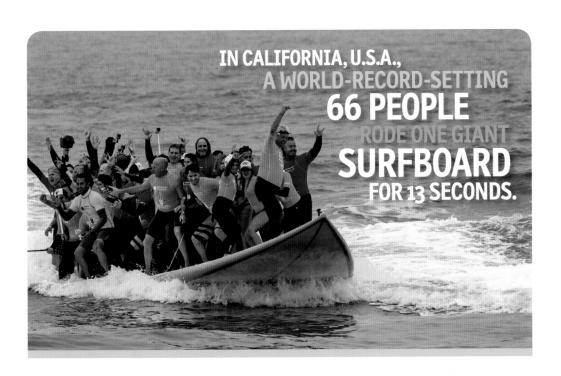

IN CALIFORNIA, U.S.A., A WORLD-RECORD-SETTING **66 PEOPLE** RODE ONE GIANT **SURFBOARD** FOR 13 SECONDS.

In the annual **Man vs. Horse race, humans** try to outrun **horses** across more than **20 miles** (32 km) of Welsh countryside.

Splash-diving competitors do **cannonballs off tall platforms** to see who can make the **biggest splash.**

Football player **Troy Polamalu's hair** was once insured for **one million dollars.**

129

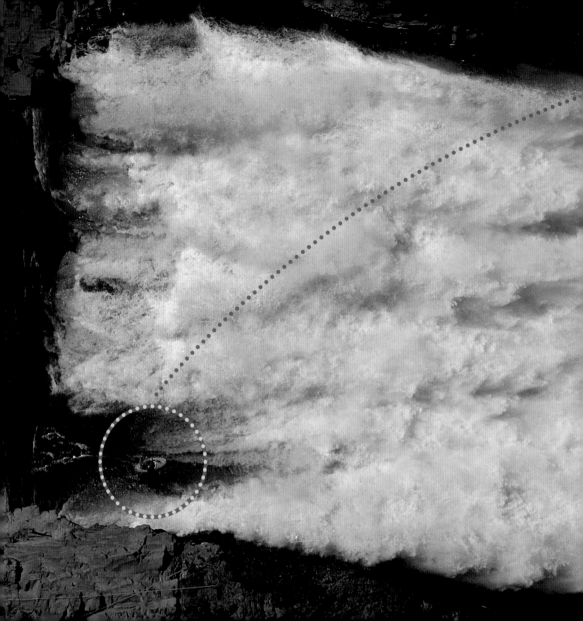

AN EXTREME KAYAKER PLUMMETED A RECORD-SETTING
18 STORIES DOWN A WATERFALL—AND LIVED!

A former **stray cat** jumped a record-breaking **6 feet**—(1.8 m) the longest leap made by a feline.

THE LONGEST PROFESSIONAL **TENNIS MATCH** LASTED 11 HOURS AND 5 MINUTES— AND PLAYED OUT OVER **3 DAYS.**

People in Lake Tomahawk, Wisconsin, U.S.A., play baseball in snowshoes— during the summer.

TWO MEN ONCE SET A WORLD RECORD BY PASSING A **GIANT** INFLATABLE **VOLLEYBALL** BACK AND FORTH **583 TIMES** WITHOUT LETTING IT TOUCH THE GROUND.

BOWLING DATES BACK TO **3200 B.C.**

DURING ONE SEASON A PRO BASKETBALL PLAYER **ATE A PEANUT BUTTER AND JELLY SANDWICH** EXACTLY 55 MINUTES BEFORE EACH GAME.

SOME ATHLETES WEAR FRUIT-PUNCH-FLAVORED MOUTH GUARDS.

Some **skateboarders** practice their moves in empty **swimming pools** and giant water pipes.

AN 11-YEAR-OLD FIGURE SKATER SPUN AT **342 REVOLUTIONS** PER MINUTE, SETTING A **WORLD RECORD** FOR FASTEST SPIN.

THE FRONT WALL OF A **JAI ALAI COURT** IS MADE OF **GRANITE—**

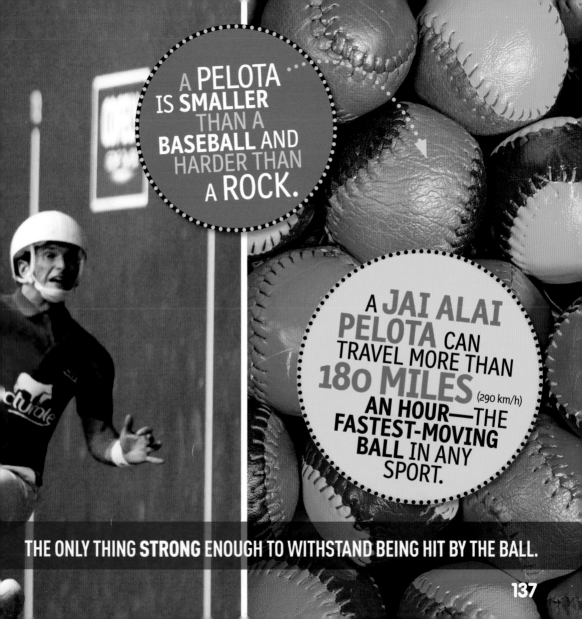

A PELOTA IS **SMALLER** THAN A **BASEBALL** AND HARDER THAN A **ROCK**.

A **JAI ALAI PELOTA** CAN TRAVEL MORE THAN **180 MILES** (290 km/h) **AN HOUR**—THE **FASTEST-MOVING BALL** IN ANY SPORT.

THE ONLY THING **STRONG** ENOUGH TO WITHSTAND BEING HIT BY THE BALL.

Half-pipes have been carved by **lava flows** at a ski resort near an active **volcano** in Chile.

THE TEMPERATURE INSIDE A SPEEDING RACE CAR CAN SOAR ABOVE 140°F. (60°C)

GAME OVER IS THE NAME **CAVERS** GAVE TO THE **DEEPEST SPOT** REACHED IN THE **DEEPEST CAVE** ON **EARTH.**

Baseball's **home plate** used to **be round** and **made of iron.**

A New Zealand woman set a world record running **100-meter hurdles** while wearing **swim fins.**

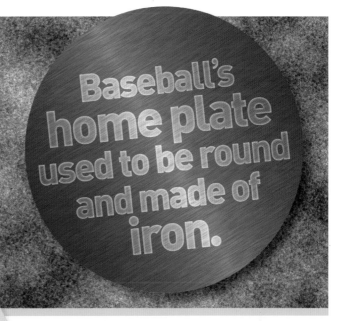

AUSTRALIANS CELEBRATE AUSTRALIA DAY BY RACING "DUNNIES"—PORTABLE TOILETS ON WHEELS.

AT AN ANNUAL EVENT IN NORTH CAROLINA, U.S.A., PEOPLE **RUN 2.5 MILES,** (4 km) EAT A **DOZEN DOUGHNUTS,** AND RACE BACK TO WHERE THEY STARTED.

A WORLD-RECORD-HOLDING **RACEWALKER** SPED ALONG AT **8.8 MILES AN HOUR—** (14 km/h) FASTER THAN MOST JOGGERS CAN JOG.

At the **Greasy Pole** competition, people try to walk the length of a horizontal slicked-up **telephone pole** without falling into the water **below.**

141

SKiJORING=
SKiiNG
WHILE HOLDING ON TO
A ROPE
ATTACHED TO A
GALLOPING
HORSE.

A **woman** once rode a **hot air balloon 41,300 feet** (12,588 m) into the air before **hang gliding** back down.

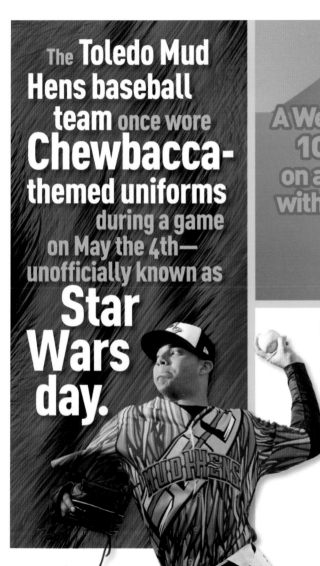

The **Toledo Mud Hens baseball team** once wore **Chewbacca-themed uniforms** during a game on May the 4th—unofficially known as **Star Wars day.**

A Welsh man rode **106 miles** (170 km) on a **unicycle** without stopping.

One art museum has a collection of **31,000** baseball cards.

x

145

In an **underwater marathon** in Pennsylvania, U.S.A., people ran on **treadmills** submerged in tanks of water.

A GERMAN MAN **ROLLER-SKATED** **5,341.3 MILES** (8,596 km) IN JUST OVER THREE MONTHS— THE LONGEST JOURNEY MADE ON SKATES.

THE **JAPANESE** SPORT OF *BO-TAOSHI*
(POLE TOPPLING)
REQUIRES 300 PEOPLE TO PLAY.

THE STONES USED IN CURLING ARE MADE FROM A TYPE OF GRANITE FOUND ONLY IN SCOTLAND.

CURLING STONES WEIGH MORE THAN A SIX-YEAR-OLD.

A SCORELESS ROUND OF CURLING IS CALLED A BLANK END.

Teams from across America compete in the **U.S. Quidditch World Cup**— inspired by the **fictional sport** in the Harry Potter books.

Participants make **"mud angels"** during Germany's Wattoluempiade (Mud Olympics).

A SAN ANTONIO SPURS FAN IN CHINA MADE A PORTRAIT OF BASKETBALL PLAYER BORIS DIAW OUT OF 11,750 PUSHPiNS.

There's a **gymnast** who can do a **double backflip** and land in a **pair of pants.**

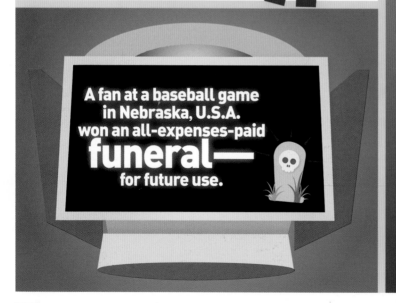

A fan at a baseball game in Nebraska, U.S.A. won an all-expenses-paid **funeral—** for future use.

THERE WAS A SQUASH COURT **ABOARD THE *TITANIC.***

Jumpy the dog cruised **328 feet** (100 m) **on a skateboard** in a record-setting **19.65 seconds.**

WACKY SPORTS SLANG

BONK=
TO RUN OUT OF STEAM DURING A GAME OR LONG WORKOUT.

CHOCOLATE CHIPS=
CLUSTERS OF ROCKS POKING OUT OF THE SNOW ON SKI SLOPES.

154

BULGE IN THE ONION BAG=
SCORING A GOAL IN SOCCER.

CAN OF CORN=
AN EASY CATCH BY A FIELDER IN BASEBALL.

FARTLEK=
A TYPE OF RUNNING WORKOUT THAT VARIES SPEED AND INTENSITY.

WATER POLO PLAYERS ONCE RODE ON TOP OF FLOATING BARRELS PAINTED TO LOOK LIKE HORSES.

WOK RACERS SIT IN BOWL-SHAPED COOKING PANS AND PLUNGE DOWN **ICY CHUTES** AT SPEEDS OF UP TO **60 MILES** (96.5 km/h) **AN HOUR.**

A PROFESSIONAL BASEBALL PLAYER ONCE HIT A **FLY BALL 560 FEET** (171 m) IN THE **AIR—** THAT'S HIGHER THAN THE SPACE NEEDLE IN SEATTLE, WASHINGTON, U.S.A.!

IN 1943 THE PHILADELPHIA **EAGLES** AND PITTSBURGH **STEELERS** FOOTBALL TEAMS MERGED TO BECOME

THE STEAGLES—

FOR ONLY ONE SEASON.

A pro baseball player once celebrated his 100th home run by running the bases backward.

PRO HOCKEY CHAMPS

HAVE PUT THEIR BABIES

INSIDE THE STANLEY CUP.

DIVERS CAN EARN MONEY FROM DREDGING UP LOST BALLS FROM THE BOTTOM OF PONDS ON GOLF COURSES.

AN ESTIMATED 100 MILLION MISSING GOLF BALLS ARE RECOVERED IN THE UNITED STATES EVERY YEAR.

AN ITALIAN MAN CAN HOLD 27 GOLF BALLS IN ONE HAND — A WORLD RECORD.

An extreme **unicyclist** pedaled along the **Great Wall of China.**

At the 2006 **Olympic opening** ceremony in **Turin, Italy, in-line skaters** crossed the stage **with flames shooting out of their helmets.**

U.S. PRESIDENTS
FRANKLIN D. ROOSEVELT,
DWIGHT EISENHOWER, RONALD REAGAN,
AND GEORGE W. BUSH WERE ALL
FORMER CHEERLEADERS.

The biggest **bony fish** ever caught using a rod and reel was a **black marlin** that weighed more than a **dairy cow.**

Tennis pros once played **a match** on top of one of the **world's tallest buildings—** about **696 feet** (212 m) above the ground.

A MAN **PLAYING DARTS** ONCE HIT A RECORD-SETTING **11 BULL'S-EYES** IN ONE MINUTE.

A MAN IN ILLINOIS, U.S.A., **JUGGLES TENNIS BALLS** WITH **ONE HAND** WHILE **THROWING DARTS** WITH THE OTHER.

THE **FEATHERS** ON A DART ARE CALLED **FLIGHTS** OR **FLETCHING**.

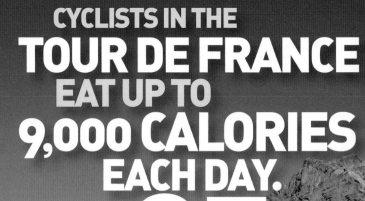

CYCLISTS IN THE
TOUR DE FRANCE
EAT UP TO
9,000 CALORIES
EACH DAY.
THAT'S LIKE EATING **25**
CHEESEBURGERS.

A RUNNING TRACK IN CHINA WAS PAINTED WITH RIGHT ANGLES INSTEAD OF CURVES.

A TABLE TENNIS BALL SHOT OUT OF AN AIR-POWERED CANNON BROKE THE SOUND BARRIER.

Surya Bonaly is the only *figure skater* to have landed a **backflip** on just **one skate.**

The first ice skates were made with animal bones.

Jetsprint boats travel up to **80 miles an hour** (129 km/h) and have **roll cages** in case the **driver** flips over.

JETSPRINT BOAT
RACERS HAVE TO
CHANGE DIRECTION
APPROXIMATELY
30 TIMES
IN LESS THAN
A MINUTE.

173

DURING ONE MAJOR LEAGUE BASEBALL GAME, A BALL BOUNCED OFF AN OUTFIELDER'S HEAD AND OVER THE FENCE FOR A HOME RUN.

A pro hockey player dunked his stick **in the toilet** before each game for good luck.

In **Segway polo,** players hit a **ball** while riding motorized two-wheel scooters instead of horses.

HOSE PULLING, STAIR CLIMBING, AND DUMMY DRAGGING ARE EVENTS IN THE ULTIMATE FIREFIGHTER COMPETITION.

In the Asian sport of *sepaktakraw* **you can hit the ball across the net with any part of your body— except your hands or arms.**

A FOOTBALL PLAYER HAS A **REPLICA OF HIS JERSEY MADE** ENTIRELY OUT OF CANDY.

TURKEY BOWLERS *HURL* A FROZEN TURKEY AT THEIR PINS.

IT'S TRADITION FOR THE WINNER OF THE INDIANAPOLIS 500 TO GUZZLE A BOTTLE OF MILK AFTER THE RACE.

Tennis superstar **Andre Agassi's** **ponytail** was once on **display** at a restaurant in **New York City.**

Speed skiers can travel faster than a **skydiver falling** to Earth in a belly-down position.

Professional basketball games have been delayed by **bats** that flew around the court.

Squash gets its name from its soft "squashable" balls.

UNICYCLE FOOTBALL TEAMS TRY TO SCORE TOUCHDOWNS WHILE PEDALING AROUND A **PARKING LOT.**

You can go **white-water rafting** in a two-billion-year-old **crater** in South Africa.

BOISTEROUS FANS CELEBRATING A **FOOTBALL GAME** IN SEATTLE, WASHINGTON, U.S.A., ONCE TRIGGERED A SMALL **EARTHQUAKE.**

A **108-YEAR-OLD WOMAN** WAS THE OLDEST PERSON EVER TO THROW OUT THE FIRST PITCH AT A MAJOR LEAGUE BASEBALL GAME.

Every year **adults race** each other down a curvy San Francisco, California, **street**—on **Big Wheels.**

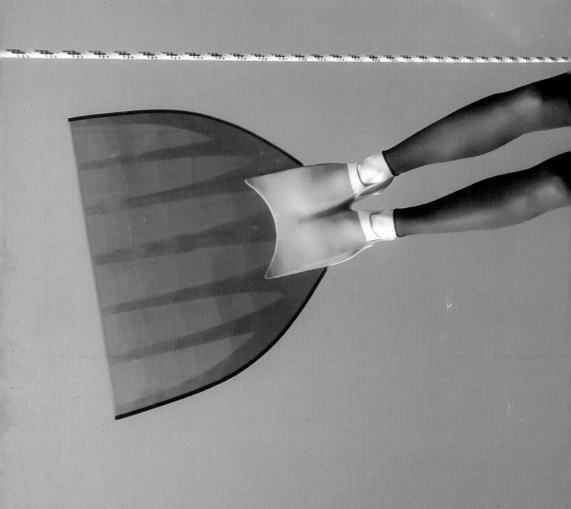

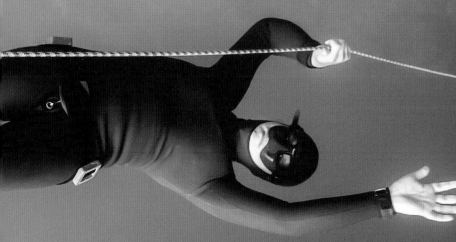

Professional **free divers** can plunge up to **656 feet** (200 m) on a single breath of air—deeper than twice the height of the Statue of Liberty.

A PROFESSIONAL BASEBALL PITCHER WAS ONCE SIDELINED FOR THREE GAMES AFTER STRAINING HIS WRIST PLAYING A VIDEO GAME.

A HIGH SCHOOL ATHLETE CAUGHT A **FOOTBALL** ONE-HANDED— WHILE DOING A BACKFLIP.

A Brazilian soccer player **shaved his head** to look like a **soccer ball.**

A BIRD ONCE STOLE A PROFESSIONAL GOLFER'S BALL DURING A COMPETITION.

DURING A MINOR LEAGUE
BASEBALL GAME
IN ILLINOIS, U.S.A., A

SKUNK

SCURRIED ONTO
THE FIELD, RAN
AROUND, AND
DUCKED OUT
THROUGH THE
LEFT-CENTER-
FIELD GATE.

THE CHICAGO BULLS MASCOT USED A SLINGSHOT TO FIRE BILLIONAIRE RICHARD BRANSON AT A SET OF **OVERSIZED BOWLING PINS.**

An **astronaut** aboard the International Space Station took **photos** of **Major League Baseball stadiums** from **space.**

SUMO WRESTLERS BEGIN MATCHES BY RINSING THEIR MOUTHS WITH WATER AND TOSSING SALT IN THE AIR.

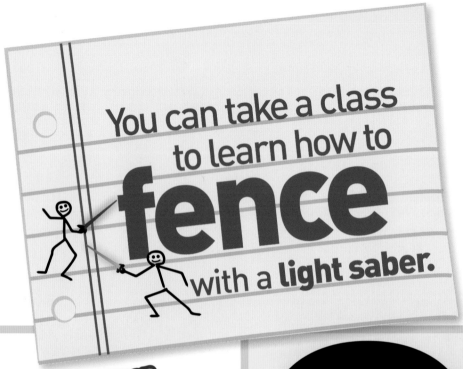

You can take a class to learn how to **fence** with a **light saber.**

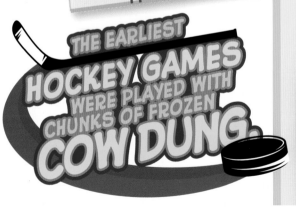

THE EARLIEST HOCKEY GAMES WERE PLAYED WITH CHUNKS OF FROZEN COW DUNG.

SQUASH MATCHES ARE PLAYED IN NEW YORK CITY'S GRAND CENTRAL TERMINAL.

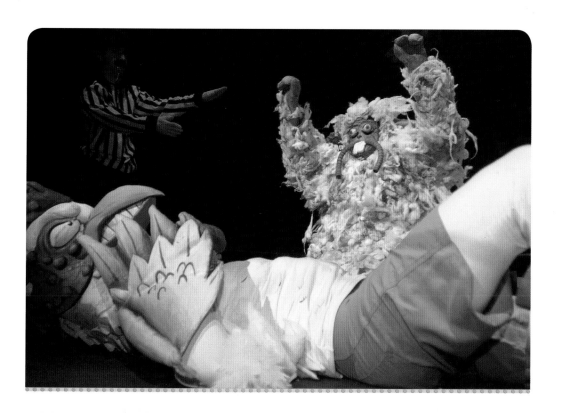

Kaiju Big Battel participants wrestle in monster costumes.

A PRO HOCKEY PLAYER ONCE LOST TEN TEETH AFTER TAKING A PUCK TO THE FACE DURING A GAME.

*Every player on **England's Liverpool Football Club** signed their names on a* **superfan's car.**

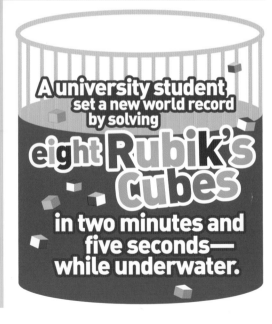

A university student set a new world record by solving **eight Rubik's Cubes** in two minutes and five seconds— while underwater.

IN SWAMP SOCCER, TEAMS **PLAY IN THICK, KNEE-DEEP** MUD

FOWLING COMPETITORS
THROW A FOOTBALL TO KNOCK DOWN AN OPPONENT'S BOWLING PINS.

Freestyle motocross rider Robbie "Maddo" Maddison performed a **no-handed backflip** across the open span of London, England's **Tower Bridge.**

THROWBACK SPORTS

BACK IN THE DAY, SOME GAMES WENT BY DIFFERENT NAMES.

GOSSIMA = PING PONG

MUSH BALL = SOFTBALL

SHOVILLABORDE = SHUFFLEBOARD

SIDEWALK SURFING = SKATEBOARDING

PLANK GLIDING = WATERSKIING

MINTONETTE = VOLLEYBALL

FACTFINDER

Boldface indicates illustrations.

200

FACTFINDER

FACTFINDER

Since 1888, the National Geographic Society has funded more than 14,000 research, conservation, education, and storytelling projects around the world. National Geographic Partners distributes a portion of the funds it receives from your purchase to National Geographic Society to support programs including the conservation of animals and their habitats. To learn more, visit natgeo.com/info.

For more information, visit www.natgeo.com/info, call 1-877-873-6846, or write to the following address:
National Geographic Partners, LLC
1145 17th Street N.W.
Washington, D.C. 20036-4688 U.S.A.

For librarians and teachers:
nationalgeographic.com/books/librarians-and-educators

More for kids from National Geographic:
natgeokids.com

National Geographic Kids magazine inspires children to explore their world with fun yet educational articles on animals, science, nature, and more. Using fresh storytelling and amazing photography, Nat Geo Kids shows kids ages 6 to 14 the fascinating truth about the world—and why they should care.
kids.nationalgeographic.com/subscribe

For rights or permissions inquiries, please contact National Geographic Books Subsidiary Rights: bookrights@natgeo.com

Design by Rachael Hamm Plett, Moduza Design
Art direction by Julide Obüz Dengel

The publisher would like to thank Jen Agresta for her efficient project management style and expert editing of this book, Hillary Leo of Royal Scruff for her keen photo editing skills, and Sarah Wassner Flynn and Alison Stevens for hitting it out of the park with their research and writing of these truly wild and wacky sports facts.

Paperback ISBN: 978-1-4263-2467-3
Library Binding ISBN: 978-1-4263-2468-0

Printed in China
21/PPS/4

Stay in the Game!

From archery to zip lining, discover **EVERYTHING** you always wanted to know about dozens of the world's favorite sports—history, training, rules and regs, play guide, and more, plus photos, facts, and fun!

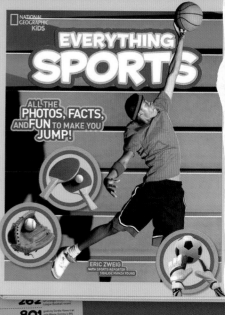